Ghent – A Travel Guide of Art and History

A comprehensive guide to the art and architecture of Ghent, Belgium

Maxime Jensens

© Maxime Jansens 2016

All rights reserved. No text of this publication may be reproduced, distributed, or transmitted in any form or by any means, including photocopying, recording, or other electronic or mechanical methods, without the prior written permission of the publisher, except in the case of brief quotations embodied in critical reviews and certain other non-commercial uses permitted by copyright law.

This book features the work of several independent, private photographers and artists. Where appropriate, they have been attributed for their work. Images used under any Creative Commons and GNU free license remain under their respective licenses. No copyright or trademark infringement is intended by the imagery displayed within this book.

Cover image credit: Simonly

Acknowledgments

I would chiefly like to thank my tutor and friend Pierre Durand for fostering my interest and knowledge in the representation of history in civic buildings. The many tour guides, tourism bureau clerks, and individuals I have encountered during my tours of the country I am proud to call my home also deserve due credit for their illuminating advice. Finally, I appreciate the help rendered by administrators of Ghent's respective fine arts attractions, whose clarifications were invaluable in the completion of this guide.

About the Author

Growing up in Brussels, Maxime Jensens developed a keen interest and sense of the historic legacies which underpin the towns of his nation. As a child, he beheld the many stunning achievements in architecture and art, whether they be on the parts of institutions such as the Christian church or individually prolific artists, sculptors or architects. Noting how these beautiful attributes seldom fail to awe visitors with their uniqueness, Jensens ambitiously aimed to make a career from their depiction, accurately relaying of the past which so underpins his home nation.

Formerly a student of art history, Jensens today acts as a lecturer and blogger studying the old cities of both Belgium and France. Fluent in both French and English, his stated aim is to increase the awareness, appreciation and regard for his country's art. It is to this end that this guide was published, for the benefit of visitors eager to plunge into the cultural bulwarks Belgium has to offer.

Introduction

The object and plan of this series of city guides is somewhat different from that of any other guides presently available. They do not compete or clash with such existing works; they are rather intended to supplement than to supplant them. My purpose is not to direct the stranger through the streets and squares of a Flemish town towards the buildings or sights which he may desire to visit; still less is it my intention to give him practical information about hotels, taxi fares, trains, tramways, and other every-day visiting conveniences. For such details, the traveller must still have recourse to the trusty pages of other, more general and utilitarian guides.

My desire rather is to supply the tourist who wishes to use his travel as a means of culture with such historical and antiquarian information as will enable him to understand, and therefore enjoy the architecture, sculpture, painting, and minor arts of the towns he visits. In one word, it is my object to give the reader in a very compendious form the result of all those inquiries which have naturally suggested themselves to my own mind during thirty-five years of foreign travel, the solution of which has cost myself a good deal of research, thought, and labour, beyond the facts which I could find in the everyday tour guide handbooks.

For several years past I have devoted myself to collecting and arranging material for a set of books to embody the idea I had thus entertained. I earnestly hope they may meet a want on the part of tourists, especially Americans, who, so far as my experience goes, usually come to Europe with an honest and reverent desire to learn from the Old World whatever of value it has to teach them, and who are prepared to take an amount of pains in turning their trip to good account which is both rare and praiseworthy. For such readers I shall call attention at times to other sources of information.

Ghent Graslei panorama - Image: Marc Ryckaert

This guide book will deal more particularly with the city of Ghent where heritage architecture, objects of art and other antiquities are numerous. In every one of them, the general plan pursued will be somewhat as follows. First will come the inquiry why the town ever gathered together at all at that particular spot—what induced the aggregation of human beings rather there than elsewhere.

Next, we shall consider why Ghent grew to social or political importance and what the stages were by which it assumed its present shape. Thirdly, we shall ask why it gave rise to that higher form of handicraft which we know as Art, and towards what particular arts it especially gravitated. After that, we shall take in detail the various strata of its growth or development, examining the buildings and works of art which they contain in historical order, and, as far as possible, tracing the causes which led to their evolution. In particular, we shall lay stress upon the origin and meaning of each structure as an organic whole, and upon the allusions or symbols which its fabric embodies.

A single instance will show the method upon which I intend to proceed better than any amount of general description. A church, as a rule, is built over the body or relics of a particular saint, in whose special honour it was originally erected. That saint was usually one of great local importance at the moment of its erection, or was peculiarly implored against plague, foreign enemies, or some other pressing and dreaded misfortune. In dealing with such a church I endeavour to show what the circumstances were which led to its construction, and what memorials of these circumstances it still retains. In other cases it may derive its origin from some special monastic body—Benedictine, Dominican, Franciscan—and may therefore be full of the peculiar symbolism and historical allusion of the order who founded it.

In dealing with a church, I try as far as possible to exhibit the effect which its origin had upon its architecture and decoration; to trace the image of the patron saint in sculpture or stained glass throughout the fabric; and to set forth the connection of the whole design with time and place, with order and purpose. In short, instead of looking upon monuments of the sort mainly as the product of this or that architect, I look upon them rather as material embodiments of the spirit of the age—crystallizations, as it were, in stone and bronze, in form and colour, of great popular enthusiasms.

By thus concentrating attention on what is essential and important in a town, I hope to give in a comparatively short space, though with inevitable conciseness, a fuller account than is usually given of the chief architectural and monumental works of the principal art-cities.

Ghent structures, with the Old Post Office to the right - Image: Michal Osmenda

As regards the character of the information given, it will be mainly historical, antiquarian, and, above all, explanatory. I am not a connoisseur—an adept in the difficult modern science of distinguishing the handicraft of various masters, in painting or sculpture, by minute signs and delicate inferential processes. In such matters, I shall be well content to follow the lead of the most authoritative experts. Nor am I an art-critic—a student versed in the technique of the studios and the dialect of the modeling-room. In such matters, again, I shall attempt little more than to accept the general opinion of the most discriminative judges. What I aim at rather is to expound the history and meaning of each work—to put the intelligent reader in such a position that he may judge for himself of the aesthetic beauty and success of the object before him. To recognise the fact that this is a Perseus and Andromeda, that a St. Barbara enthroned, the other an obscure episode in the legend of St. Philip, is not art-criticism, but it is often an almost indispensable prelude to the formation of a right and sound judgment. We must know what the artist was trying to represent before we can feel sure what measure of success he has attained in his representation.

I cannot venture to hope that handbooks containing such a mass of facts as these will be wholly free from errors and misstatements. I can only beg those who may detect any such to point them out, without unnecessary harshness, to the author, care of the publisher, and if possible to assign reasons for any dissentient opinion.

Table of Contents

Acknowledgments 3
About the Author 4
Introduction 5
How to Use this Guidebook 11
Origins of the Belgian Towns 13
Ghent 22
    Origins of Ghent 23
    The Core of Ghent 29
    Saint Bavo's Cathedral 44
        Lower Tier 54
        Upper Tier 58
    The City and Outskirts of Ghent 65
        Ghent Museum of Fine Arts 75
Historical Notes on Belgium 80

How to Use this Guidebook

As noted already, the guidance within this book does not profess to supply practical information in aid of transport, dining, accommodation, guided tours or general sightseeing, but rather is intended to enlighten the visitor about the old town and interesting items of culture, history and art said locale harbours. As such, it is best suited as a companion to a more general guidebook, enhancing and conferring depth in matters artistic and cultural.

You can happily read this book at leisure at home prior to your journey to Ghent. The sections upon specific art galleries or cathedrals however are best read while you explore and view each respective building and its contents. Individual artworks and artifacts are described, while descriptions upon their creators also feature.

Portions relating to each principal objects of art should be quietly read and digested before a visit, and referred to again afterwards. The portion to be read on the spot is made as brief as possible. For eBook readers it is advised to read with a large font size so as to be easily read in the dim light of churches, chapels, and galleries. Those with editions in print may benefit from reasonably sized, 12 point fonts. Where objects are numbered, the numbers used are always those of the latest official catalogues.

Individual works of merit are distinguished by an asterisk (*); those of very exceptional interest and merit have two asterisks. Undistinguished art of little notability is omitted, so that the tourist may appreciate works of renown.

As for touring advice, you should little at a time, and see it thoroughly. Never attempt to "do" any place or any monument in a quick, whirlwind tour characterized by brief milling around. By following strictly the order in which objects are noticed in this book, you will gain a conception of the historical evolution of the town which you cannot obtain if you go about looking at churches and palaces haphazardly.

This book does not profess to be an exhaustive account of the art and architecture present in Belgian cities. Its focus is mainly on the ancient heritage art and architecture of the medieval, renaissance and baroque periods, which together span epochs between the 12th and 18th century. These fruitful centuries birthed much of the best and most beautiful Belgian art and architecture, the styles of which remain with ease the most associated with the country and each of its significant cities.

Clearer memories, enjoyment and appreciation of the architecture and art of Belgium's principle art galleries and churches is what this book intends to convey, in contrast to ordinary guides which lack focus and depth upon the important historical and cultural characteristics of the cities they focus upon. Where they merely brush over art of supreme importance, as if ticking boxes off a list – this book aims to interest the artistic tourist with due description and intensity.

In aid of this aim parts relating directly to the old town, galleries, church and cathedral interiors, this book acts as a walking tour. Concise descriptions and instructions are made, enlightening you as to when to stop and observe specific items of significance.

Origins of the Belgian Towns

The somewhat heterogeneous country which we now call Belgium formed part of Gaul under the Roman Empire. But though rich and commercial even then, it seems to have been relatively little Romanised; and in the beginning of the 5th century it was overrun by the Salic Franks, on their way towards Laon, Soissons, and Paris. When civilization began to creep northward again in the 9th century through the districts barbarised by the Teutonic invasion, it was the Frankish Charlemagne (Karl the Great) who introduced Roman arts afresh into the Upper and Lower Rhinelands.

The Rhine from Basle to Cologne was naturally the region most influenced by this new Roman revival; but as Charlemagne had his chief seat at Aix-la-Chapelle (Aachen), near the modern Belgian frontier, the western Frankish provinces were also included in the sphere of his improvements. When the kingdom of the Franks began to divide more or less definitely into the Empire and France, the Flemish region formed nominally part of the Neustrian and, later, of the French dominions. From a very early date, however, it was practically almost independent, and it became so even in name during its later stages. But Brabant (with Brussels) remained a portion of the Empire.

The Rhine constituted the great central waterway of mediæval Europe; the Flemish towns were its ports and its manufacturing centres. They filled in the 13th and 14th centuries much the same place that Liverpool, Glasgow, Manchester, and Birmingham fill in the 20th. Many causes contributed to this result. Flanders, half independent under its own Counts, occupied a middle position, geographically and politically, between France and the Empire; it was comparatively free from the disastrous wars which desolated both these countries, and in particular (see under Ghent) it largely escaped the long smouldering quarrel between French and English which so long retarded the development of the former. Its commercial towns, again, were not exposed on the open sea to the attacks of pirates or hostile fleets, but were safely ensconced in inland flats, reached by rivers or canals, almost inaccessible to maritime enemies. Similar conditions elsewhere early ensured peace and prosperity for Venice.

An ancient canal running through rural Belgium - Image: Arctic-Cycler

The canal system of Holland and Belgium began to be developed as early as the 12th century (at first for drainage), and was one leading cause of the commercial importance of the Flemish cities in the 14th. In so flat a country, locks are all but unnecessary. The two towns which earliest rose to greatness in the Belgian area were thus Bruges and Ghent; they possessed in the highest degree the combined advantages of easy access to the sea and comparative inland security. Bruges, in particular, was one of the chief stations of the Hanseatic League, which formed an essentially commercial alliance for the mutual protection of the northern trading centres. By the 14th century Bruges had thus become in the north what Venice was in the south, the capital of commerce. Trading companies from all the surrounding countries had their "factories" in the town, and every European king or prince of importance kept a resident minister accredited to the merchant Republic.

Some comprehension of the mercantile condition of Europe in general during the Middle Ages is necessary in order to understand the early importance and wealth of the Flemish cities. Southern Europe, and in particular Italy, was then still the seat of all higher civilization, more especially of the trade in manufactured articles and objects of luxury. Florence, Venice, and Genoa ranked as the polished and learned cities of the world. Further east, again, Constantinople still remained in the hands of the Greek emperors, or, during the Crusades, of their Latin rivals. A brisk trade existed viâ the Mediterranean between Europe and India or the nearer East. This double stream of traffic ran along two main routes—one, by the Rhine, from Lombardy and Rome; the other, by sea, from Venice, Genoa, Florence, Constantinople, the Levant, and India.

On the other hand, France was still but a half civilized country, with few manufactures and little external trade; while England was an exporter of raw produce, chiefly wool. The Hanseatic merchants of Cologne held the trade of London; those of Wisby and Lübeck governed that of the Baltic; Bruges, as head of the Hansa, was in close connection with all of these, as well as with

Hull, York, Novgorod, and Bergen. The position of the Flemish towns in the 14th century was thus not wholly unlike that of New York, Philadelphia, and Boston at the present day; they stood as intermediaries between the older civilized countries, like Italy or the Greek empire, and the newer producers of raw material, like England, North Germany, and the Baltic towns.

The Hunt of Maximilian tapestry

The local manufactures of Flanders consisted chiefly of woolen goods and linens; the imports included Italian luxuries, Spanish figs and raisins, Egyptian dates, Oriental silks, English wool, cattle, and metals, Rhenish wines, and Baltic furs, skins, and walrus tusks.

In the early 16th century, when navigation had assumed new conditions, and trade was largely diverted to the Atlantic, Antwerp, the port of the Schelde, superseded the towns on the inland network. As Venice sank, Antwerp rose.

The art that grew up in the Flemish cities during their epoch of continuous commercial development bears on its very face the visible impress of its mercantile origin. France is essentially a monarchical country, and it is centralized in Paris; everything in old French art is therefore regal and lordly. The Italian towns were oligarchies of nobles; so the principal buildings of Florence and Venice are the castles or palaces of the princely families, while their pictures represent the type of art that belongs in its nature to a cultivated aristocracy.

But in Flanders, everything is in essence commercial. The architecture consists mainly, not of private palaces, but of guilds, town halls, exchanges, belfries: the pictures are the portraits of solid and successful merchants, or the devotional works which a merchant donor presented to the patron saint of his town or business. They are almost overloaded with details of fur, brocade, jewelry, lace, gold, silver, polished brass, glasswork, Oriental carpets, and richly carved furniture. In order to understand Flemish art, therefore, it is necessary to bear in mind at every step that it is the art of a purely commercial people.

Another point which differentiates Flemish painting from the painting of Italy during the same period is the complete absence of any opportunity for the display of frescoes. In the Italian churches, where the walls serve largely for support, and the full southern light makes the size of the windows of less importance, great surfaces were left bare in the nave and aisles, or in the lower part of the choir, crying aloud for decoration at the hands of the fresco-painter. But in the northern Gothic, which aimed above all things at height and the soaring effect, and which almost annihilated the wall, by making its churches consist of rows of vast windows with intervening piers or buttresses, the opportunity for mural decoration occurred but seldom.

The climate also destroyed frescoes. Hence the works of pictorial art in Flemish buildings are almost confined to altar-pieces and votive tablets. Again, the great school of painting in early Italy (from Giotto to Perugino) was a school of fresco-painters; but in Flanders no high type of art arose till the discovery of oil-painting. Pictures were usually imported from the Rhine towns. Hence, pictorial art in the Low Countries seems to spring almost full-fledged, instead of being traceable through gradual stages of evolution as in Italy. Most of the best early paintings are small and highly finished; it was only at a comparatively late date, when Antwerp became the leading town, that Italian influence began to produce the larger and coarser canvases of Rubens and his followers.

Very early Flemish art greatly resembles the art of the School of Cologne. Only with Hubert and Jan van Eyck (about 1360-1440)

does the distinctively Flemish taste begin to show itself—the taste for delicate and minute workmanship, linked with a peculiar realistic idealism, more dainty than German work, more literal than Italian. It is an art that bases itself upon truth of imitation and perfection of finish: its chief æsthetic beauty is its jewel-like colour and its wealth of decorative adjuncts. The subsequent development of Flemish painting—the painting that pleased a clique of opulent commercial patrons—we shall trace in detail in the various cities.

Whoever wishes to gain a deeper insight into Flemish painting should take in his portmanteau Sir Martin Conway's "Early Flemish Artists," a brilliant and masterly work of the first importance, to which this Guide is deeply indebted.

The political history of the country during this flourishing period of the Middle Ages has also stamped itself, though somewhat less deeply, on the character of the towns and of the art evolved in them. The Counts of Flanders, originally mere lords of Bruges and its district, held their dominions of the Kings of France. Their territory included, not only Arras (at first the capital, now included in France) with Bruges, Ghent, Courtrai, Tournay, and Ypres, but also the towns and districts of Valenciennes, Lille, and St. Omer, which are now French. From the time of Baldwin VIII. (1191), however, Arras became a part of France, and Ghent was erected into the capital of Flanders. In the beginning of the 13th century, two women sovereigns ruled in succession; under them, and during the absence of the elective Counts on crusades, the towns rose to be practically burgher republics. Bruges, Ypres, Ghent, and Lille were said to possess each 40,000 looms; and though this is certainly a mediæval exaggeration, yet the Flemish cities at this epoch were at any rate the chief manufacturing and trading centres of northern Europe, while London was still a mere local emporium.

A statue of Jacob van Artevelde - Image: Demeester

In the 14th century, the cities acquired still greater freedom. The citizens had always claimed the right to elect their Count; and the people of Ghent now made treaties without him on their own account with Edward III. of England. To this age belongs the heroic period of the Van Arteveldes at Ghent, when the burghers became the real rulers of Flanders, as will be more fully described hereafter. In 1384 however, Count Louis III died, leaving an only daughter, who was married to Philip the Bold of Burgundy; and the wealthy Flemish towns thus passed under the sway of the powerful princes of Dijon. Brabant fell later by inheritance to Philip the Good. It was under the Burgundian dynasty, who often held their court at Ghent, that the arts of the Netherlands attained their first great development. Philip the Good (1419-1467) employed Jan van Eyck as his court painter; and during his reign or just after it the chief works of Flemish art were produced in Bruges, Ghent, Brussels, and Tournai.

Charles the Bold, the last Duke of Burgundy, left one daughter, Mary, who was married to Maximilian, afterwards Emperor. From that date forward the history of the Flemish towns is practically merged in that of the dynasty of Charles V., and finally becomes the story of an unwilling and ever justly rebellious Spanish province. The subsequent vicissitudes of Belgium as an Austrian appanage, a part of Holland, and an independent kingdom, belong to the domain of European history. For the visitor, it is the period of the Burgundian supremacy that really counts in the cities of Belgium.

Yet the one great point for the tourist to bear in mind is really this—that the art of the Flemish towns is essentially the art of a group of burgher communities. It is frankly commercial, neither royal nor aristocratic. In its beginnings it develops a strictly municipal architecture, with a school of painters who aimed at portraiture and sacred panel pictures. After the Reformation had destroyed sacred art in Holland, painting in that part of the Netherlands confined itself to portraits and to somewhat vulgar popular scenes: while in Belgium it was Italianised, or rather Titianised and Veronesed, by Rubens and his followers. But in its best days it was national, local, and sacred or personal.

Take Conway's "Early Flemish Artists" with you in your portmanteau, and read over in the evening his account of the works you have seen during the day.

Ghent

A Panoramic view of Ghent - Image: Michael Schmalenstroer

The modern Ghent is an attractive and commonly overlooked city and capital of East Flanders. Somewhat overshadowed by its close neighbor Bruges, Ghent as city nevertheless boasts a greater size and scope with its civic contours bending around the one uniting feature of Flanders – its waterways.

Picturesque scenes and architecture may be beheld alongside the River Leie, with the old city centre and Graslei locality of great interest to visitors. As well as the majestic scenes unfolding in the centre, the enchanting gothic spires of the city's cathedral and old town.

Recent modernization of the tramways and bus system have made navigation easier. Owing to this and steady promotional efforts, tourist numbers continue to trend upward. Many visitors, privy to the fact the town's social, economic and religious heritage are so intertwined with its architectural achievements and beauty, are keen to absorb the many artistic works and designs which populate the major attractions.

Origins of Ghent

Flanders owes everything to its water communications. At the junction of the Schelde with the Lys or Lei, there grew up in the very early Middle Ages a trading town, named Gent in Flemish, and Gand in French, but commonly Anglicised as Ghent. It lay on a close network of rivers and canals, formed partly by these two main streams, and partly by the minor channels of the Lieve and the Moere, which together intersect it into several islands. Such a tangle of inland waterways, giving access to the sea and to Bruges, Courtrai, and Tournai, as well as less directly to Antwerp and Brussels, ensured the rising town considerable importance in early eras.

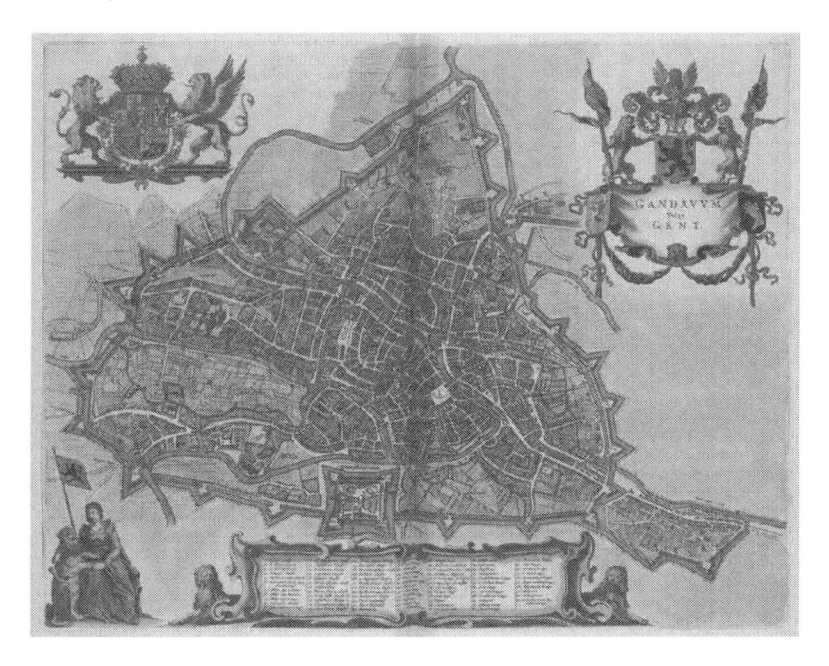

It formed the centre of a radiating commerce. Westward, its main relations were with London and the English wool ports;

eastward with Cologne, Maastricht, the Rhine towns, and Italy. Ghent was always the capital of East Flanders, as Bruges or Ypres were of the Western province; and after the Counts lost possession of Arras and Artois, it became in the 13th century their principal residence and the metropolis of the country. The trade in weaving grew rapidly in importance, and the Ghenters received from their Count a charter of liberties of the usual mediæval burgher type.

Battle of the Spurs sketch from the Royal Society of Antiquaries depicting an engagement of militia and cavalry

As time went on, and the city advanced in wealth, its subjection to its sovereigns became purely nominal. Ghent equipped large bodies of citizen soldiers, and repulsed a considerable English army under Edward I. The Ghenters were also determined opponents of the claims of the French kings to interfere in the internal affairs of Flanders; thus they were mainly instrumental in winning the famous Battle of the Spurs in 1302, when the citizens of Bruges and Ghent put to flight the army of France under the Count of Artois before the walls of Tournai, and dedicated as trophies 700 golden spurs, worn by the French knights whom they had routed. This battle, memorable as one of the chief triumphs of nascent industrial freedom over the chivalry and royalty of medievalism, secured the liberties of the Flemish towns against French aggression.

Early in the 14th century, the burghers of Ghent, under their democratic chief, Jacob or Jacques Van Artevelde, attained practical independence. Till 1322, the Counts and people of Flanders had been united in their resistance to the claims of France; but with the accession of Count Louis of Nevers, the aspect of affairs changed. Louis was French by education, sympathies, and interests, and aristocratic by nature; he sought to curtail the liberties of the Flemish towns, and to make himself despotic. The wealthy and populous burgher republics resisted, and in 1337 Van Artevelde was appointed Captain of Ghent. Louis fled to France, and asked the aid of Philip of Valois.

Thereupon, Van Artevelde made himself the ally of Edward III. of England, then beginning his war with France; but as the Flemings did not like entirely to cast off their allegiance—a thing repugnant to medieval sentiment—Van Artevelde persuaded Edward to put forward his trumped-up claim to the crown of France, and thus induced the towns to transfer their fealty from Philip to his English rival. It was therefore in his character as King of France that Edward came to Flanders. The alliance thus formed between the great producer of raw wool, England, and the great manufacturer of woollen goods, Ghent, proved of immense commercial importance to both parties. But as Count Louis sided with Philip of Valois, the breach between the democracy of Ghent and its nominal sovereign now became impassable. Van Artevelde held supreme power in Ghent and Flanders for nine years—the golden age of Flemish commerce—and was treated on equal terms by Edward, who stopped at Ghent as his guest for considerable periods. But he was opposed by a portion of the citizens, and his suggestion that the Black Prince, son of Edward III., should be elected Count of Flanders, proved so unpopular with his enemies that he was assassinated by one of them, Gerard Denys. The town and states immediately repudiated the murder; and the alliance which Van Artevelde had brought about still continued. It had far-reaching results; the woollen industry was introduced by Edward into the Eastern Counties of England, and Ghent had risen meanwhile to be the chief manufacturing city of Europe.

The sun sets over the river Lys in Ghent - Image: Graham Richter

The quarrel between the democratic weavers and their exiled Counts was still carried on by Philip van Artevelde, the son of Jacques, and godson of Queen Philippa of England, herself a Hainaulter. Under his rule, the town continued to increase in wealth and population. But the general tendency of later medieval Europe towards centralised despotisms as against urban republics was too strong in the end for free Ghent. In 1381, Philip was appointed dictator by the Democratic Party, in the war against the Count, son of his father's old opponent, whom he repelled with great slaughter in a battle near Bruges. He then made himself Regent of Flanders. But Count Louis obtained the aid of Charles VI. of France, and defeated and killed Philip Van Artevelde at the disastrous battle of Roosebeke in 1382. That was practically the end of local freedom in Flanders. Though the cities continued to revolt against their sovereigns from time to time, they were obliged to submit for the most part to their Count and to the Burgundian princes who inherited from him by marriage.

The subsequent history of Ghent is that of the capital of the Burgundian Dukes, and of the House of Austria. Here the German king, Maximilian, afterwards Emperor, married Mary of Burgundy, the heiress of the Netherlands; and here Charles V. was born in the palace of the Counts. It was his principal residence, and he was essentially a Fleming. Other historical reminiscences will be pointed out in the course of our peregrinations.

The old waterways, partially artificial, between Ghent and the sea, other than the circuitous route by the shallow Schelde, had silted up by 1827, when a ship canal was constructed to Terneuzen. This canal has since been widened and deepened so as to admit vessels of 1,700 tons; for a time this helped to some small degree to save the town from the commercial decline suffered by Bruges. In the 21st century however, it took several enhancements of the port and sea facilities in order for the city to retain its commercial reputation. But as its mouth lies in what is now Dutch territory, and as heavy tolls are levied, it is comparatively little used. Another and somewhat frequented canal leads to Bruges; but Ghent owes most of its existing prosperity to its manufactures (cotton, linen, engines, leather) and to its central position on the railway system.

The important points for the tourist to bear in mind are these, however. Ghent during the Middle Ages was a merchant republic, practically independent, with its guilds and its belfry, the last of which was used to summon the citizens to arms in case of danger. It was also the chief manufacturing town in Europe, as Bruges was the chief commercial centre. By treaty with Edward III., Bruges was made the "staple" or sole port of entry for English wool: and this wool was woven into cloth for the most part at Ghent.

Further details of the vicissitudes of Ghent can be found in Van Duyse, Gand, Monumental et Pittoresque.

The chief objects of interest at Ghent are the Cathedral, with its great Van Eyck; and the Town Hall and Belfry. These can be tolerably seen in one day: but a stay of three or four days will not be too much to explore the curious nooks of the early city.

The Core of Ghent

The old town of Ghent lies on the island formed by the junction of the Lys and the Schelde, with their various backwaters (all now largely artificial). Near this point, but beyond the Lys, the Counts of Flanders early erected a strong castle, the Gravensteen or Oudeburg, beneath whose protection, aided by the two navigable rivers, merchants and weavers gradually settled. As at Bruges, the heart of the town, however, is purely municipal and mercantile in its architecture. The Town Hall, which was the meeting-place of the citizens, and the Belfry, which summoned them to arms or council, are the chief points of interest in the city. The Schelde is still tidal to its very centre.

A vibrant market takes place in The Kouter - Image: Demeester

As many visitors will probably stop in one of the hotels on the the Kouter, near the southern end of older Ghent, I shall frankly take that square as our starting-point. Formerly termed the Place D'Armes, The Kouter is an ideal base from which to explore the greater city. To the right of The Kouter is swiftly sighted the large square tower; that of the Cathedral, while the tapering spire, crowned by a gilt dragon, belongs to the Belfry.

Go first on a tour of orientation through early Ghent. If you follow these directions implicitly, you can see everything important in one short walk. Cross the Kouter diagonally to the northeast corner, and follow the small and narrow streets which run due north to the front of the Cathedral. Walk round the south side of this, to form a first general impression, but do not enter it at present.

Exterior of St. Bavos Cathedral - Image: Mylius

Then, from the West Front of the Cathedral, take the Rue St. Jean straight before you. The tower with the gilded dragon which faces you as you walk is that of the Belfry. It was designed in 1183, about a century earlier than that of Bruges, but only erected between 1321 and 1339; it is a fine work in the Early Gothic style. Its windows have been walled up. The tapering turret which crowns the tower is unfortunately modern, and of iron. On the very summit stands a huge gilded dragon, which universal tradition represents as having been brought from St. Sophia at Constantinople to Bruges by the Crusader Baldwin of Flanders, (1204), and removed as a trophy by the people of Ghent (under Philip van Artevelde) in 1382. It certainly appears to be of Oriental origin, but is stated on documentary evidence (discovered by M. Vuylsteke) to have been made in Ghent itself in 1380. If so, it would seem at least to be based on an Oriental model.

Ghent Belfry and cloth hall - Image: Donarreiskoffer

The relatively small building at the foot of the Belfry, is the Cloth Hall, erected in 1424, a graceful but not very important Gothic edifice (of the Decorated period), with niches vacant of their statues. The concierge of the Belfry now has a room in it, with entry possible upon request.

The view is extensive and beautiful, but not quite so striking as that at Bruges. The principal buildings of the city lie just below you: beyond, all Flanders. The chimes are celebrated. The chief bell is known as Roelandt.

The Botermarkt in Ghent - Image: Demeester

Now turn round into the Botermarkt or Marché au Beurre to the right, and inspect the Belfry again from the little bay in the corner opposite. This is the best near view of the tower. The portal to the right was formerly the entry to the town prison, beneath the Belfry, now in course of complete restoration. In its gable is a too-famous 18th century relief (the Mammelokker) representing the Roman daughter feeding her father from her breast at the window of a prison, and doubtless intended to excite the charity of passers-by. It certainly serves no other function, for it is neither beautiful nor decorative.

The Mammelokker depicts a Roman named Pero, a prisoner, breast-fed by his daughter to ward off starvation.

Cross over to the right side of the market. The building on the left, in two totally distinct portions, is the Hôtel-de-Ville. The part at which you first arrive, (latest in point of time,) was rebuilt in the early Renaissance style in 1595-1628. It is one of the earliest and in many ways the best example of Renaissance architecture in Belgium, in part because it retains certain good features of local domestic building, such as the pointed gable-ends (round the corner to the left) and the projecting windows with dormers on the main façade. (Look out for their origin elsewhere.) It has three storeys, with projecting half colonnades, the columns being Doric on the ground floor, Ionic on the first floor, and Corinthian on the second. Recollect the gable-ends and dormers for comparison with others in old houses in Ghent hereafter.

Now, continue on to the corner, where we arrive at the earlier Gothic portion of the Hôtel-de-Ville, erected in 1518-1535 by Dominic de Waghemakere, who also built in part the cathedral at Antwerp. The projecting polygonal corner, with its handsome balcony, is very noticeable. The work is of the latest and most florid Gothic, somewhat lacking in grace and dignity, but ornate in its splendour. Observe the depressed arches, the noble cornice, the rich decoration of garlands. A few of the niches have now been filled with modern statues of saints. From the corner opposite, a good view is obtained of both parts of the Hôtel-de-Ville and also of the Belfry.

Turn to the left into the Rue Haut-Port, to observe the main front of this earlier Gothic building, with its fine projecting windows above, its empty niches, its handsome entrance staircase and main portal, its beautiful little balcony for addressing the people below, and the large projecting window of its ancient chapel near the centre. Note how well the façade is thus broken up and diversified. This is the finest specimen of florid Gothic in Belgium. Beyond it comes another Renaissance portion, and then a handsome Renaissance dwelling-house. The street also contains several fine early houses, the best of which (a Gothic guildhall, known as the Cour St. Georges) stands at the corner to the left, facing the Hôtel-de-Ville.

The interior of the Hôtel-de-Ville need not be visited, though it has a handsome Gothic staircase (demolished, sold, built into a private house, re-erected) and some fine halls and internal courts, interesting to those who have plenty of time at their disposal.

Now, return to the Belfry and continue straight down the left-hand side of the Rue de la Catalogne. The church on the right, round the base of which houses have been allowed to cluster, is St. Nicolas—the oldest in the town. This is one of the most solid pieces of architecture at Ghent. It has a fine decorated tower, which has happily escaped restoration, besides small turrets to the Transepts, and two, rather larger, to the gable of the Nave.

The ever-lively Korenmarkt - Image: PMRMaeyaert

Go on into the Koornmarkt or Marché aux Blés, to the right; stand there for a moment, at the end of the Rue de la Catalogne, to observe the fine coup d'œil, which takes in St. Nicolas, the Belfry, and the tower of the Cathedral. The main façade of St. Nicolas faces the Koornmarkt. Over the door is a modern figure of the Saint himself, raising the three boys who were salted down for meat. Nicolas was the popular saint, the patron of the merchants and burgesses; and the prominent position of his church on the Corn Market is very characteristic of the burgher spirit of Ghent.

A hasty glance will suffice for the interior, which is a characteristic specimen of the Belgian church, with figures of the Twelve Apostles, as always, against the pillars of the Nave; an ugly carved pulpit; short Transepts; an Apse with bad glass; and the vaulting of Nave, Aisles, and Choir concealed by plaster. The tawdry decorations render what might be a fine interior wholly unimpressive. The High Altar has an altar-piece by Liemakere, representing, in the confused style of the School of Rubens, the election of St. Nicholas as Bishop of Myra. Above is an 18th century figure of the Saint, raising the three boys from the tub. The early pillars of the Choir are really handsome.

On emerging from the front of the church, continue straight on to the bridge which crosses the Lys, affording a good view to the left of the Apse of St. Michel. Then, go along the side of this handsome church, with late Gothic windows resembling English Perpendicular. It has a solid but unfinished tower, and a good West Portal, robbed of its sculpture and cruelly mutilated. A glimpse at the interior, which has been scraped and renovated, will show at once the fine architecture. The Nave has impressive round pillars, windows in the clerestory, and excellent brick vaulting. The vaulted Aisles are surrounded by chapels.

The Choir is very handsome. Walk round the Transepts and Ambulatory. There are some good works of the School of Rubens.

Now, continue along the quay, on the same side as St. Michel, (observing as you go that the early town extended to both banks of the river), in order to view the façade of the handsome Maison des Bateliers, or Guild House of the Skippers, erected in 1531 for the masters of the shipping of Ghent, in somewhat the same florid late-Gothic style as the Hôtel-de-Ville. This is the finest existing specimen of old Flemish houses. Over the doorway is an appropriate relief of a ship, somewhat antiquated and heraldic in character. By the side of this Guild-house are two others, less interesting: the first, the Guild House of the Grain Measurers; the next, very old and dilapidated, the Staple House of Corn, Romanesque, said to be the earliest civil building in Belgium. Several fine gable-ends are seen to the left, including one with Renaissance architecture, on this side of the Lys. At the moment of writing, the houses next to the Skippers' Guild are in course of demolition, exposing a bare side of the old Hall most unpicturesquely.

Now, retrace your steps over the Bridge, and through the Corn Market, almost wholly modernized, with the exception of a few gabled houses.

Cafe terraces at the Grande Boucherie - Image: Stephane Mignon

The next little square at which we arrive is the Marché aux Herbes. Its W. side is occupied by the ancient but uninteresting Grande Boucherie. Turn to the left by the corner of the

Boucherie, with Our Lady and Child in a niche, and cross the bridge to the other side of the Lys. On the left are two handsome old houses. In front rise the gateway and bastions of the Oudeburg, or Castle of the Princes. This was the primitive palace of the Counts of Flanders in Ghent.

The castle has recently been cleared from the numerous modern houses which encumbered and hid it. The first stronghold on this site was erected in 868. The existing ruins of the gateway, with round Romanesque arches, date back to 1180; the square keep behind is of the 10th century. In this palace Jacob van Artevelde entertained Edward III. When Edward returned to England, he left Queen Philippa here, and during his absence she bore (in the Monastery of St. Bavon) her third son, John of Gaunt, who took his well-known surname from the place of his birth. It was on Edward's return to Flanders, accompanied by the ladies of Philippa's suite, that he found the French fleet drawn up near Sluys to prevent his entry into the port of Bruges, on which occasion he gained the first great English naval victory. The Castle, which is now in course of partial restoration, is closely bound up with the greatness of Van Artevelde and the heroic period in the history of Ghent.

Walk round it to note its extent and its commanding position at the point where the bridge crosses the Lys to the main part of the town.

The opposite corner of the c has a Renaissance gateway, re-erected in imitation of the original by Arthus Quellin, and adorned with sculptures of Neptune, the Schelde, and the Lys, the sources of Ghent's greatness. It leads to the Fish-market. Around are several good old houses.

Continue along the quay on the same side of the river as the Oudeburg, as far as the Pont du Laitage, just before reaching which you pass on your left two 17th century houses with reliefs, (the Works of Charity, a Flying Hart, etc.). Cross the bridge and turn to the right as far as the big cannon, known as Dulle Griete or Mad Margaret, dating back to the 14th century. By the touch-hole are the Cross of St. Andrew and the Arms of Phillipe le Bon of Burgundy.

Turn into the large square in front of you. The building which faces you at the end of the street as you advance (with a tower at the corner and high gables) is one of the best old medieval houses in Ghent, the Collacie-Zolder, or Municipal Council-Room, of the 13th or 14th century. It has an interesting little pulpit or balcony at its corner, with a bell, from which addresses could be made to the people. The towers that face you a little to the left are those of St. Jacques, to be visited presently.

Statue of Jacob van Artevelde in Vrijdagmarkt - Image: David Huang

Continue into the square, at the corner of which is the Municipal Council-Room. This is the Vrijdagmarkt or Marché du Vendredi, in which a strikingly picturesque market is still held every Friday morning. If possible, visit it. The square was the forum of old Ghent and the meeting-place of the citizens. A few fine old buildings in the native local style still surround it. The centre is appropriately occupied by a modern colossal statue of Jacob van Artevelde, addressing the citizens in his famous speech when he excited them to opposition to the Count of Flanders with his Gallicising policy. At the base are allegorical figures of Flanders, and of the Belgian towns, wearing mural crowns.

The reliefs represent Van Artevelde's three chief diplomatic triumphs,—the League of Ghent with Bruges and Ypres; the League of Flanders and England; the League of Flanders, Brabant, and Hainault. In this square the most important events in the history of early Flanders took place. Here the citizens of Ghent took the oath of allegiance to each new Count on his accession, after they had compelled him to swear in good old Teutonic style "to uphold and see upheld all the standing wits (laws), fore-rights (regulations), freehoods, and wonts of the Countship and town of Ghent."

The guilds which had their halls around met here to oppose arbitrary action on the part of their sovereign. Here, too, the parties within the town itself frequently joined issue in civil contest. In later times, the Duke of Alva perpetrated most of his shameful executions on this spot. The site of the statue of Van Artevelde was originally occupied by one of Charles V., who was born in Ghent, in a palace now destroyed, and whose history (see later) is intimately connected with this town, always one of his principal residences. The statue was destroyed in 1794 by the French invaders: (picture in the Museum).

St. James Church exterior - Image: Paul Hermans

Turn up at the corner by the Municipal Council-Room and take the first street to the left, which leads you into the Place St. Jacques, occupied by the Church of St. Jacques. The façade, with the two towers, was Romanesque, but has been restored in such a wholesale way as to destroy its interest. The remainder of the church is Gothic. Walk round it so as to observe its features, noticing in particular the quaint stone spire of the right-hand tower.

The interior might be good, were it not spoiled by tawdry decorations. The pulpit has a marble figure of the patron, St. James, with the pilgrim's staff and gourd, emblematic of his connection with the great place of pilgrimage of Santiago de

Compostella. The vaulting has been freed from excrescences, and is excellent of its kind. The High Altar has a figure of St. James above, and a painting of his martyrdom beneath.

This walk will have led you through the principal part of early Ghent. Hence you may return either by the Cathedral, or by the chief line of business streets which runs direct from the Pont du Laitage to the modern Palais de Justice and the Place d'Armes.

Saint Bavo's Cathedral

[Official website: http://www.sintbaafskathedraal.be/

Opening hours are between 9:30am and 5pm during the summer season, while during the winter season from the hours of 10:30pm to 4pm. Year round on Sundays the chapel is open from 1pm until the evening.

An ordinary visit and tour costs 4 Euros, with discounted rates available for groups and students.

There is an audio guide available which explains some of the artworks within the premises.]

The local patron saint of Ghent is St. Bavo, a somewhat dubious personage, belonging to the first age of Christianity in Flanders, of whom little is known.

Legend describes him as a "Duke of Brabant" in the 7th century, which is of course an anachronism. He seems to have been a nobleman of Hesbaie who spent his life as a soldier "and in worldly pleasures"; but when he was 50, his wife died. Overwhelmed with grief, he gave up all his possessions to be distributed among the poor, and entered a cell or monastery in Ghent, of which St. Amand (see later) was the founder. Of this he became abbot.

Saint Bavo's Cathedral exterior - Image: Michal Osmenda

At last, finding the monastic life not sufficiently austere, the new saint took refuge in a hollow tree in a forest, and there spent the remainder of his days. His emblem is a falcon. The monastery of St. Bavon long existed at Ghent; some of its ruins still remain, and will be described hereafter. To this local saint, accordingly, it might seem fitting that the Cathedral of Ghent should be dedicated. But in reality the building first functioned as a parish church under the invocation of St. John the Baptist, and only received the relics and name of St. Bavon after 1540, when Charles V. destroyed the monastery, as will be described hereafter.

The real interest of the Cathedral centres, however, not in the ruins of St. Bavon, nor in his picture by Rubens, but in the great polyptych of the Adoration of the Lamb, the masterpiece of Jan van Eyck and his brother Hubert, which forms in a certain sense the point of departure for the native art of the Netherlands. This is therefore a convenient place in which to consider the position of these two great painters. They were born at Maaseyck or Eyck-sur-Meuse near Maastricht; Hubert, the elder, about 1360 or 1370; Jan, the younger, about 1390.

Ruins of the Virgin's crypt - St. Bavon's Abbey

The only undoubted work of Hubert is the altar-piece in St. Bavon, and even this is only his in part, having been completed after his death by his brother Jan. Hubert probably derived his teaching from the School of the Lower Rhine, which first in the North attained any importance, and which had its chief exponents at Maastricht and Cologne. Of this School, he was the final flower. Though not, as commonly said, the inventor of oil-painting, he was the first artist who employed the process in its developed form, and he also made immense advances in naturalness of drawing and truth of spirit.

Jan was probably a pupil of Hubert; he lived at Ghent while the great picture of the Adoration of the Lamb was still being completed; later, he was painter by appointment to the court of the Dukes of Burgundy, and had a house at Bruges, where he died in 1440. He was also employed on various missions abroad, accompanying embassies as far as to Portugal. His painting, though less ideal and beautiful than that of his great successor Memling, is marvellous in its truth: it has an extraordinary charm of purity of colour, vividness of delineation, and fine portrayal of character. Indeed, all the early Flemish artists were essentially portrait painters; they copied with fidelity whatever was set before them, whether it were fabrics, furniture, jewellery, flowers, or the literal faces and figures of men and women.

Hubert and Jan van Eyck, however, were not so much in strictness the founders of a school as the culminating point of early German art, to which they gave a new Flemish direction. Their work was almost perfect in its own kind. Their successors did not surpass them: in some respects they even fell short of them.

The Adoration of the Lamb is by far the most important thing to be seen at Ghent. But it is viewed at some disadvantage in the church, and is so full of figures and meaning that it cannot be taken in without long study. I strongly advise you, therefore, to buy a photograph of the entire composition beforehand, and try to understand as much as possible of the picture by comparing it with the account here given, the evening before you visit the picture. You will then be able more readily to grasp the actual work, in form and colour, when you see it.

Go straight from your hotel to the Cathedral,—built as the parish church of St. John about 1250-1300; re-dedicated to St. Bavon, 1540; erected into a Bishop's see, 1599. Stand before the West Front at a little distance, to examine the simple but massive architecture of the tower and façade.

The great portal has been robbed of the statues which once adorned its niches. Three have been "restored": they represent, centre, the Saviour; on the left is the patron, St. Bavon, recognisable by his falcon, his sword as duke, and his book as monk; he wears armour, with a ducal robe and cap above it; right, St. John the Baptist, the earlier patron.

Then, walk, to the right, round the south side, to observe the external architecture of the Nave, Aisles, and Choir. The latter has the characteristic rounded or apsidal termination of Continental Gothic, whereas English Gothic has usually a square end. Enter by the S. portal.

The interior, with single Aisles and short Transepts, (Early Gothic) is striking for its simple dignity, its massive pillars, and its high arches, though the undeniably noble effect of the whole is somewhat marred to English eyes by the unusual appearance of the unadorned brick walls and vaulting. The pulpit, by

Delvaux (1745), partly in oak, partly in marble, represents Truth revealing the Christian Faith to astonished Paganism (figured as an old and outworn man:) it is a model of all that should be avoided in plastic or religious art. The screen which separates the Choir from the Transepts is equally unfortunate. The apsidal end of the Choir, however, with its fine modern stained glass, forms a very pleasing feature in the general coup d'œil.

Begin the examination in detail with the left or north Aisle. The 1st chapel, that of the Holy Cross, contains a Pietà by Janssens and a Descent from the Cross by Rombouts, good works of the school of Rubens. The 3rd chapel, that of St. Macarius or St. Macaire (an object of local worship whom we shall meet again elsewhere at Ghent), has a modern statue of the saint, and a pleasing decoration in polychrome. The right or S. Aisle has nothing of importance.

A short flight of steps leads to the Ambulatory, whose black-and-white marble screen, on the side toward the Choir, is not without dignity.

The sacristan opens the locked Chapels in the Ambulatory (flamboyant), beginning at the steps on the right or south side of the Choir. You will find him in the Sacristy, in the N. Transept. Do not let him hurry you.

The 1st chapel contains a tolerable triptych by F. Pourbus (son of Peter), with the Finding of Christ in the Temple for its central subject, and the Circumcision and Baptism on the inner wings. Notice in the last the conventional attitudes of the Baptist, the Saviour, and the angel with the towel, as in the Gerard David and all old examples of this subject: but the semi-nude figure undressing in the foreground is an unhappy innovation of the Renaissance. Many of the heads in the central picture are portraits: Alva, Charles V., Philip II., and Pourbus himself. On the outer wings is a good *portrait of the donor (Viglius) adoring the Saviour (1571).

3rd chapel. Crucifixion, by Gerard van der Meire, of Ghent. On the left wing, Moses striking the Rock, symbolical of the fountain of living water, Christ. On the right wing, the Elevation of the Brazen Serpent, symbolical of the Crucifixion. This is a mystic "typical" picture, interesting only for its symbolism. Note the Flemish love of such subjects.

The 4th chapel contains a good tomb of Cornelius Jansen and Willem Lindau, the two first bishops of Ghent (bishopric founded only in 1599) with fair recumbent figures of the early 17th century.

5th chapel. Coxcie. Lazarus and Dives: a mediocre picture.

Mount the steps to the Upper Ambulatory.

The 6th chapel (of the Vydts family) contains the famous altarpiece of the **Adoration of the Lamb, by Hubert and Jan van Eyck, to study which is the chief object of a visit to Ghent. See it more than once, and examine it carefully. Ask the Sacristan to let you sit before it for some time in quiet, or he will hurry you on. You must observe it in close detail.

St Bavo's Cathedral interior and ceilings - Image: Michal Osmenda

As a whole, the work before you is not entirely by the two Van Eycks. The Adam and Eve on the outer upper shutters of the interior (originally by Hubert) have been altogether removed, and are now in the Museum at Brussels, where we shall see them in due course. Their place has been filled, not by copies (for the originals were nude), but by skin-clad representations of the same figures, whose nudity seemed to the Emperor Joseph II. unsuitable for a church. The lower wings, which were principally (it is believed) by Jan van Eyck, have also been removed, and sold to Berlin. They are replaced by very tolerable copies, made in the early 16th century by Michael Coxcie. Thus, to form an idea of the detail of the original in its full totality it is necessary to visit, not only Ghent, but also Brussels and Berlin. Nevertheless, I describe the whole picture here as it stands, as this is the best place to observe its general composition. I shall say a few words later as to variations of this work from the original. There is a good copy of the whole picture in the Museum at Antwerp, where you will be able to inspect it at greater length and under easier conditions. The remaining portions of the original still left here are believed to be for the most part the work of Hubert van Eyck. Jan must rather be studied in many scattered places,—Bruges, Brussels, Berlin, Paris, Madrid, and London.

The altar-piece was commissioned from Hubert van Eyck by Josse Vydts (Latinised as Jodocus), a gentleman of Ghent, and his wife, Isabella, about the year 1420. Hubert died while the polyptych was still unfinished, and Jan completed it in 1432. Too much importance has been attached by critics, I fancy, to the rhyming hexameter inscribed upon it, (with the words "De Eyck" unmetrically introduced:) "Pictor Hubertus major quo nemo repertus," etc. They have been twisted into a deliberate expression of belief on the part of Jan that Hubert was a greater painter than himself. If so, it seems to me, Jan was a worse critic than painter. They are probably due, however, to a somewhat affected modesty, or more probably still, to a priestly poet who was in straits to find a rhyme for Hubertus.

I proceed to a detailed explanation of the picture.

The subject, in its entirety, is the Adoration of the Lamb that was Slain, and it is mainly based on the passage in the Apocalypse: "I looked, and lo, a Lamb stood on the Mount Zion, and with Him an hundred and forty and four thousand, having His Father's name written in their foreheads. . . . And I heard the voice of harpers harping with their harps." Elsewhere we read: "I beheld, and, lo, a great multitude, which no man could number, clothed with white robes, and palms in their hands. . . . These are they which came out of great tribulation, and have washed their robes, and made them white in the blood of the Lamb. Therefore are they before the throne of God; and He shall feed them, and shall lead them to living fountains of waters, and shall wipe away all tears from their eyes." Much of the imagery, however, I believe, is also taken from the Te Deum.

Lower Tier

The central panel (original: attributed to Hubert) represents in its middle the altar, hung with red damask, and covered with a white cloth, on which the Lamb of God is standing. His blood flows into a crystal chalice. (This part is clearly symbolical of the Eucharist.) Upon Him, from above, descends the Holy Ghost, in the form of a dove, sent out by the Eternal Father, who occupies the central panel on top. Around the altar are grouped adoring angels, with many-coloured wings, holding the instruments of the Passion—the Cross, the Spear, the Sponge, and the Column to which Christ was fastened for flagellation. In front of it, two angels swing censers.

The flowery foreground is occupied by the Fountain of Life, from which pure water flows limpid, to irrigate the smiling fields of Paradise. Four bands of worshippers converge towards this centre. On the left-hand side, stand, kneel, or ride, a group of worshippers representing, as a whole, the secular aspect of the Christian Church—the laity. The foreground of this group is occupied by the precursors of Christ. Conspicuous among them are the Jewish prophets in front, and then the Greek poets and philosophers,—Homer, Plato, Aristotle—whom mediæval charity regarded as inspired in a secondary degree by the Spirit of Wisdom. Homer, in white, is crowned with laurel. The group also includes kings and other important secular personages. The right-hand side, opposite, is occupied by representatives of the Church, showing the religious as opposed to the secular half of the Christian world. In the front rank kneel 14 persons, the Twelve Apostles (with Paul and Matthias) in simple robes, barefooted; behind them are ranged all the orders of the hierarchy—canonized popes, with their attendant deacons; archbishops, bishops, and other dignitaries.

The background shows two other groups, one of which (to the left) consists of the Martyrs, bearing their palms of martyrdom, and including in their number popes, cardinals, bishops, and other ecclesiastics. The inner meaning of this group is further emphasized by the symbolical presence of a palm tree behind them. To balance them on the right advance the Virgins conspicuous among whom are St. Agnes with her lamb, St. Barbara with her tower, St. Catherine, and St. Dorothy with her roses: many of them carry palms of martyrdom. These various groups thus illustrate the words of the Te Deum, representing "the glorious company of the apostles," "the goodly fellowship of the prophets," "the noble army of martyrs," "the Holy Church throughout all the world," etc., in adoration of the Lamb that was Slain. (A chorus of Apostles, of Prophets, of Martyrs, of Virgins is common in art.)

The more distant background is occupied by towered cities, typifying perhaps the New Jerusalem, but adorned with Flemish or Rhenish turrets and domes, and painted with Flemish minuteness and exactitude.

On the front of the altar are written in Latin the words, "Behold the Lamb of God that taketh away the sins of the world."

The Left Wings (inferior copy by Coxcie: originals, probably by Jan, now at Berlin) form a continuation of the scene of the Prophets and the secular side of Christendom in the central panel, and represent, in the First or Inner Half, the Orders of Chivalry and the mediæval knighthood riding, as on a crusade or pilgrimage, towards the Lamb that was Slain. At their head go the soldier saints, St. George, St. Adrian, St. Maurice, and St.

Charlemagne (for the great emperor Karl is also a canonized person). The action of the horses throughout is admirable. The Second or Outer Half (ill described as "the Just Judges") represents the Merchants and Burgesses, among whom two portraits in the foreground are pointed out by tradition as those of Hubert and Jan van Eyck: (Hubert in front, on a white horse: Jan behind, in a dark brown dress, trimmed with fur). But this detail is unimportant: what matters is the colour and composition on one hand, the idea on the other. These two panels, therefore, with the group in front of them, are to be taken as representing the Secular World—learned, noble, knightly, or mercantile—in adoration of the central truth of Christianity as manifested in the Holy Eucharist.

The corresponding Right Wings (copy by Coxcie: originals, probably by Jan, at Berlin) show respectively the Hermits and Pilgrims—the contemplative and ascetic complement of the ecclesiastical group in front of them: the monastic as opposed to the beneficed clerics. The First or Inner Half shows the Eremites, amongst whom are notable St. Anthony with his crutch, and, in the background, St. Mary Magdalen with her box of ointment, emerging from her cave, (the Sainte Baume) in Provence, in her character as the Penitent in the Desert. On the Second or Outer Half, the body of Pilgrims is led by the gigantic form of St. Christopher, with his staff and bare legs for wading; behind whom is a pilgrim with a scallop-shell, and many other figures, not all of them (to me) identifiable. Here again the presence of palms in the background marks the esoteric idea of martyrdom.

I need not call attention throughout to the limpid sky, the fleecy clouds, the lovely trees, the exquisite detail of architecture and landscape.

Upper Tier

The three Central Panels (original) are attributed to Hubert. That in the middle represents, not (I feel sure) as is commonly said, Christ, but God the Father ("Therefore they are before the throne of God") wearing the triple crown (like the Pope), holding the sceptre, and with his right hand raised in the attitude of benediction. His face is majestic, grave, passionless: his dress kingly: a gorgeous morse fastens his jewelled robe of regal red. At his feet lies the crown of earthly sovereignty. He seems to discharge the Holy Ghost on the Lamb beneath him. The word Sabaoth, embroidered on his garments, marks him, I think, as the Father: indeed, the Son could hardly preside at the sacrifice of the Lamb, even in the Eucharist.

On the right of the Father, in the panel to the (spectator's) left (Hubert: original), Our Lady, crowned, as Queen of Heaven, sits reading in her blue robe. Her face is far more graceful than is usual in Flemish art: indeed, she is the most charming of Flemish Madonnas. Behind her is stretched a hanging of fine brocade.

The panel to the right (Hubert: original) shows St. John the Baptist, with his camel-hair garment, covered by a flowing green mantle. The folds of all these draperies in Hubert's three figures, though simple, have great grandeur.

The Outer Wing to the left (substituted clothed figure, not a copy: original, by Hubert, at Brussels) has Adam, as typical (with Eve) of unregenerate humanity: a sense further marked by the Offerings of Cain and Abel above it.

The Outer Wing to the right has an Eve with the apple, (similarly clad, not copied from the original, by Hubert, now at Brussels:) above it, the First Murder.

The Inner Left Wing (copy: the original, attributed to Jan, is at Berlin) has a beautiful group of singing angels.

The Inner Right Wing (copy: the original, likewise attributed to Jan, is also at Berlin) has an angel (not St. Cecilia) playing an organ, with other angels accompanying on various musical instruments.

Taking it in its entirety, then, the altar-piece, when opened, is a great mystical poem of the Eucharist and the Sacrifice of the Lamb, with the Christian folk, both Church and World, adoring. It was in order to prepare your mind for recognition of this marked strain of mysticism in the otherwise prosaic and practical Flemish temperament, that I called your attention at Bruges to several mystic or type-emphasising pictures, in themselves of comparatively small æsthetic value.

The composition contains over 200 figures. Many of them, which I have not here identified, can be detected by a closer inspection, which, however, I will leave to the reader.

Now, ask the sacristan to shut the wings. They are painted on the outer side (all a copy) mainly in grisaille, or in very low tones of colour, as is usual in such cases, so as to allow the jewel-like brilliancy of the internal picture to burst upon the observer the moment the altar-piece is opened.

The lower wings have (in this copy) representations of the Four Evangelists, in niches, in imitation of statuary. Observe the half-classical pose and costume of Luke, the Beloved Physician. These figures, however, were not so arranged in the original, as I shall afterwards explain.

The upper wings represent on their first or lowest tier, the Annunciation, a frequent subject for such divided shutters. In the centre is the usual arcade, giving a glimpse of the town of Ghent where Hubert painted it. (The scene is said to be Hubert's own studio, which stood on the site of the Café des Arcades in the Place d'Armes: the view is that which he saw from his own windows.) To the left as always is the angel Gabriel, with the Annunciation lily; to the right is Our Lady, reading. The Dove descends upon her head. The ordinary accessories of furniture are present—prie-dieu, curtain, bed-chamber, etc. Note this arrangement of the personages of the Annunciation, with the empty space between Our Lady and the angel: it will recur in many other pictures. Observe also the Flemish realism of the painter, who places the scene in his own town at his own period: and contrast it with the mysticism of the entire conception. The uppermost tier of all is occupied by figures of two Sibyls (universally believed in the Middle Ages to have prophesied of Christ) as well as two half-length figures of the prophets Zachariah and Micah, (also as foretellers of the Virgin birth).

In several details the outer shutters in this copy differ markedly from the originals at Berlin. Jan's picture had, below, outer panels (when shut), portraits of Josse Vydts and his wife: inner panels, imitated statues (in grisaille) of St. John the Baptist and St. John the Evangelist, patrons at that time of this church. If you are going on to Berlin, you will see them: if back to London, then go to the Basement Floor of the National Gallery, where you will find the water-colour copy done for the Arundel Society, which will give you an excellent idea of the work in its original condition.

A few words must be given to the external history of this great altar-piece. It was begun by Hubert about 1420. His death in 1426 interrupted the work. Jan probably continued to paint at it till 1428, when he went to Portugal. On his return, he must have carried it to Bruges, where he next lived, and there completed it in 1432. It was then placed in this the family chapel of Josse Vydts. During the troubles of the Reformation it was carried to the Hôtel-de-Ville, but after the capitulation to the Duke of Parma it was restored to the chapel of the Vydts family.

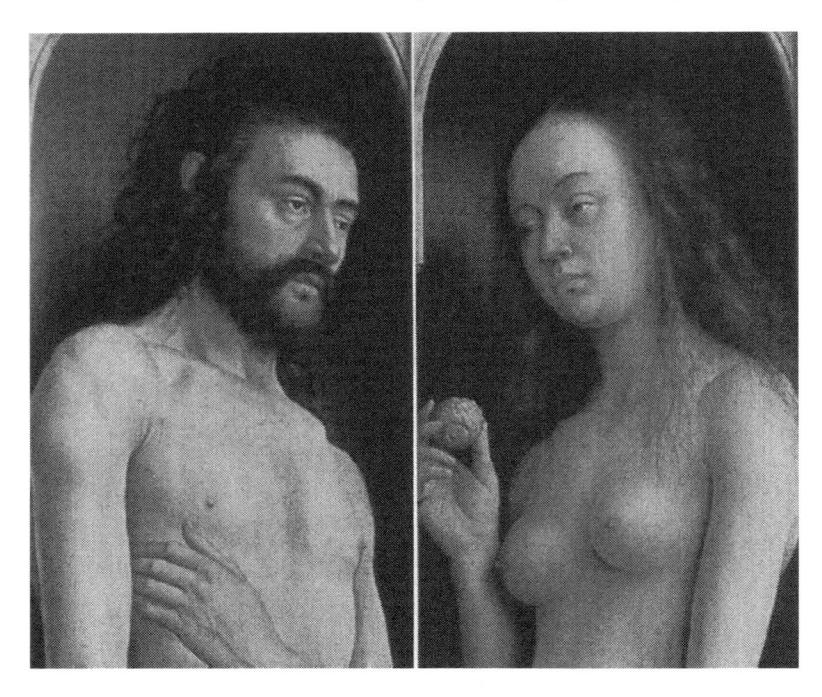

Adam and Eve

Philip II. wished to carry it off, but had to content himself with a copy by Coxcie, the wings of which are now in this chapel. The panels with Adam and Eve were removed in 1784, after Joseph II. had disapproved of them, and hidden in the sacristy. In 1794, the remaining panels were carried to Paris: after the peace, they were returned, but only the central portions were replaced in the chapel. The wings, save Adam and Eve, were sold to a Brussels dealer, and finally bought by the King of Prussia, which accounts for their presence at Berlin. As for Adam and Eve, the church exchanged them with the Brussels Museum for the wings of Coxcie's copy. These various vicissitudes will explain the existing condition of the compound picture. Do not be content with seeing it once. Go back to your hotel, rest and re-read this description, and come again to study this immortal art afresh tomorrow. The chapel of the Holy Sacrament, in the Apse, has very ugly rococo monuments to bishops of the 18th century, in the worst style of the debased Renaissance, and other monstrosities.

The 10th chapel has a famous *altar-piece by Rubens, St. Bavon renouncing his worldly goods to embrace the monastic life. The Saint is seen, attired as a Duke of Brabant of the 17th century, in his armour and ducal robes, attended by his pages, making his profession at the door of a stately Renaissance church, such as certainly did not exist in the North in his time, and received with acclamation by a dignified body of nobly-robed ecclesiastics, including St. Amand (see later, under the Monastery of St. Bavon). The features of the patron saint are said to be those of Rubens; they certainly resemble his portrait of himself at Florence. The foreground is occupied by a group of poor, to whom St. Bavon's worldly goods are being profusely scattered.

On the left are two ladies, in somewhat extravagant courtly costumes, who are apparently moved to follow the Saint's example. They are said to be the painter's two wives, but the resemblance to their known portraits is feeble. This is a fine specimen of Rubens's grandiose and princely manner, of his feeling for space, and of his large sense of colour; but it is certainly not a sacred picture. It was appropriately painted for the High Altar in the Choir (1624), after the church was dedicated to St. Bavon and erected into a cathedral, but was removed from that place of honour in the 18th century to make room for a vulgar abomination by Verbruggen. (I defer consideration of Rubens and his school till we reach Brussels and Antwerp.) Fair monument of a 17th century bishop.

Choir and altar of Saint Bavo Cathedral - Image: Edward Webster

Descend the steps again. Enter the Choir, a very fine piece of architecture: it has beautiful grey stone arches (dating to about 1300), a handsome Triforium, and excellent brick vaulting. The lower portion, however, is still disfigured by black-and-white marble screens and several incongruous rococo tombs, some of which have individual merit. (That to the left, Bishop Triest by Duquesnoy, is excellent in its own genre.) Over the High Altar flutters a peculiarly annoying and flyaway 17th century figure of the Apotheosis of St. Bavon, the patron saint of the Cathedral, who of course thus occupies the place of honour. It is by Verbruggen. The huge copper candlesticks, bearing the royal arms of England as used by Charles I, belonged to his private oratory in Old St. Paul's in London, and were sold by order of Cromwell. At this point, you can enjoy an impressive view down the Nave.

The City and Outskirts of Ghent

Old Ghent occupies for the most part the island which extends from the Palais de Justice on one side to the Botanical Gardens on the other. This island, bounded by the Lys, the Schelde, and an ancient canal, includes almost all the principal buildings of the town, such as the Cathedral, St. Nicolas, the Hôtel-de-Ville, the Belfry, and St. Jacques, as well as the chief Places, such as the Marché aux Grains, the Marché aux Herbes, and the Marché du Vendredi. It also extended beyond the Lys to the little island on which is situated the church of St. Michel, and again to the islet formed between the Lieve and the Lys, which contains the château of the Counts and the Place Ste. Pharailde.

Ghent botanical gardens

In the later middle ages, however, the town had spread to nearly its existing extreme dimensions, and was probably near as populous as it is in the 21st century. But its ancient fortifications have been destroyed, and their place has been taken by boulevards and canals. The line may still be traced on the map, or walked round through a series of shipping suburbs; but it is uninteresting to follow, a great part of its course lying through the more squalid portions of the town. The only remaining gate is that known as the Rabot (1489), a very interesting and picturesque object, situated in a particularly apartment ridden suburb. It can best be reached by crossing the bridge near the church of St. Michel, and continuing along the Rue Haute to the Boulevard du Béguinage, (where stood originally the Grand Béguinage, whose place is now occupied by modern streets.) Turn there along the boulevard to the right, till you reach the gate, which consists of two curious round towers, enclosing a high and picturesque gable-end. Owing to the unpleasant nature of the walk, I do not recommend this excursion.

The Rabot gate - Image: Traveler100

The S. quarter of the town, beyond the Cathedral and St. Nicolas has been much modernized during the last two centuries. Its only interesting points are the recent Palais de Justice and the Kouter or Place d'Armes, (once the archery ground) in which a pretty flower-market is held on Friday and Sunday mornings. The Café des Arcades, at its E. end, occupies the site of Hubert van Eyck's studio.

The rest of the inner town contains little that throws light on its origin or history.

There is, however, one small excursion which it would be well for those to take who have a morning to spare, and who desire to understand the development of Ghent—I mean to the Monastery of St. Bavon, which alone recalls the first age of the city. Every early mediæval town had outside its walls a ring of abbeys and monasteries, and Ghent was particularly rich in this respect.

St Bavos Abbey - Image: Paul Hermans

St. Amand was the apostle of Flanders and the surrounding countries. He was sent by the pious king Dagobert to convert the Flemings en bloc, and is said to have built, about 630, a little cell by the bank of the Lys, N.E. of the modern city. In 651, St. Bavon entered this infant monastery, which henceforth took his name. The abbey grew to be one of the most important in Flanders, and occupied a large area on the N.E. of the town, near the Antwerp Gate. Eginhard, the biographer and son-in-law of Charlemagne, was abbot in the 9th century. The Counts of Flanders had rights of hospitality at St. Bavon's; hence it was here, and not in the Oudeburg as usually stated, that Queen Philippa gave birth to John of Gaunt.

In 1539 however, Charles V, a headstrong despot, angry at the continual resistance of his native town to his arbitrary wishes, dissolved the monastery in the high-handed fashion of the 16th century, in order to build a citadel on the spot. As compensation for disturbance to the injured saint, he transported the relics of St. Bavon to what was then the parish church of St. John, which has ever since borne the name of the local patron. Around the dismantled ruins, the Emperor erected a great fort, afterwards known as the Spaniards' Castle, (Château des Espagnols, or Het Spanjaards Kasteel.) This gigantic citadel occupied a vast square space, still traceable in the shape of the modern streets; but no other relic of it now remains. The ruins of the Abbey are in themselves inconsiderable, but they are certainly picturesque and well worth a visit from those who are spending some days in Ghent. The hurried tourist may safely neglect them.

The direct route from the Kouter to the Abbey is by the Quai du Bas Escaut, and the Rue Van Eyck. A pleasanter route, however, is by the Rue de Brabant and the Rue Digue de Brabant to the Place d'Artevelde, passing through the handsomest part of the modern town. (In the Place itself stands the fine modern Romanesque Church of St. Anne, the interior of which is sumptuously decorated in imitation of mosaic.) Thence, follow the Quai Porte aux Vaches to the Place Van Eyck. Cross the bridges over the Upper and Lower Schelde, and the Abbey lies straight in front of you.

St. Anne's Church - Image: Limowreck

Walk past the ivy-clad outer wall of the ruins to the white house at the corner of the street beyond it, where you will find the concierge (notice above the door). The concierge conducts you over the building, which has a picturesque cloister, partly Romanesque, but mainly 15th century. The centre of the quadrangle is occupied by a pretty and neatly-kept garden of the old sweet-scented peasant flowers of Flanders. The most interesting part of the ruins, however, is the octagonal Romanesque Baptistery or, a fine piece of early vaulting, with round arches, very Byzantine in aspect. The chapel rests on massive piers, and its Romanesque arches contrast prettily with the transitional Gothic work of the cloister in the neighbourhood. Within are several fragments of Romanesque sculpture, particularly some *capitals of columns, with grotesque and naïve representations of Adam and Eve with the Lord in the Garden, and other similar biblical subjects. (Examine closely.) There is likewise an interesting relief of St. Amand preaching the Gospel in Flanders, and a man-at-arms in stone, of Artevelde's period, removed from the old coping of the Belfry.

We next go on to the Crypt, the tombs of the monks, the monastery cellars, etc., where are collected many pieces of ancient sculpture, some found in the ruins and others brought from elsewhere. The Refectory at the end, which for some time served as the Church of St. Macaire, is now in course of transformation into a local Museum of Monumental Art. It contains some good old tombs, and an early fresco (of St. Louis?) almost obliterated. But the garden and cloister are the best of the place, and make together a very pretty picture. You can return by the Quai and the Rue St. Georges, or by the Place St. Bavon and the Archiepiscopal Palace. (The castellated building to the left, much restored, near the Cathedral, known as the Steen of Gérard le Diable, is the sole remaining example of the mediæval fortified houses in Ghent.)

Another monastery, a visit to which will lead you through the extensive southern portion of the city, is the (wholly modernized) Benedictine Abbey of St. Peter's. This is open from 10am to 6pm, with a tour featuring a film available at 4 euro. To reach it, you take the Rue Courte du Jour and the Rue Neuve St. Pierre, to the large square known as the Plaine St. Pierre, partly obtained by demolition of the monastery buildings. It is situated on rising ground, which may pass for a hill in Flanders. This is, in its origin, the oldest monastery in Ghent, having been founded, according to tradition, by St. Amand himself, in 630, on the site of an ancient temple of Mercury.

The existing buildings, however, hardly date in any part beyond the 17th century. The Church of Notre-Dame de St. Pierre was erected between 1629 and 1720, in the grandiose style of the period. It is vast, and not unimposing. The interior has a certain cold dignity. The pictures are mostly of the school of Rubens, many of them dealing with St. Peter and St. Benedict; among them are good specimens. The best, by De Crayer, shows the favourite Benedictine subject of St. Benedict recognising the envoy of King Totila, who personated the king.

The Plaine de St. Pierre is used for the events on the yearly calendar, from Mi-Carême to Easter.

On the way back from the Picture Gallery, you pass on your left the Rue Longue des Pierres, down which, a little way on the right, is a small Museum of Antiquities. I do not advise a visit to this. It contains one good brass, and some silver badges worn by ambassadors of Ghent, but otherwise consists, for the most part, of third-rate bric-à-brac.

Most visitors to Ghent go to see the Grand Béguinage. This was originally situated in a little district by itself, close to the gate of the Rabot, where its church, uninteresting, (dedicated, like that of Bruges, to St. Elizabeth of Hungary), still stands; but the site has been occupied by the town for new streets. The present Grand Béguinage lies on the road to Antwerp. It is a little town in miniature, enclosed by wall and moat, with streets and houses all very neat and clean, but of no archæological interest. Yet it forms a pleasant enough end for a short drive. And you can buy lace there. The description in Baedeker is amply sufficient.

Bruges is full of memories of the Burgundian Princes. At Ghent it is the personality of Charles V., the great emperor who cumulated in his own person the sovereignties of Germany, the Low Countries, Spain and Burgundy, that meets us afresh at every turn. He was born here in 1500, and baptized in a font (otherwise uninteresting) which still stands in the north Transept of the Cathedral. Ghent was really, for the greater part of his life, his practical capital, and he never ceased to be at heart a Ghenter. That did not prevent the citizens from justly rebelling against him in 1540, after the suppression of which revolt Charles is said to have ascended the Cathedral tower, while the executioner was putting to death the ringleaders in the rebellion, in order to choose with his brother Ferdinand the site for the citadel he intended to erect, to overawe the freedom-loving city. He chose the Monastery of St. Bavon as its site, and, as we have seen, built there his colossal fortress, now wholly demolished. The Palace in which he was born and which he inhabited frequently during life, was known as the Cour du Prince. It stood near the Ancien Grand Béguinage, but only its name now survives in that of a street. The Spaniard's Castle was long the standing menace to freedom in the Low Countries. Within its precincts Egmont and Hoorn were imprisoned in 1568 for several months before their execution.

During the early Middle Ages, the Oudeburg was the residence of the Counts of Flanders in Ghent. Later on, that castellated building grew out of keeping with the splendour of the Burgundian Princes, and its place as a royal residence was taken by the Cour du Prince, already mentioned, which was inhabited by Maximilian and his wife, Mary of Burgundy, as well as by Philippe le Beau and Johanna of Spain, the parents of Charles V. No direct memorials of the great Emperor now exist in Ghent, his statue in the Marché du Vendredi having been destroyed; but a modern street commemorates his name, and mementoes of him crop up at every point in the city.

Though the Ghenters were rebellious subjects, Charles V. was proud of his capital, and several of his very bad bon mots, punning on the words Gand and gant, have been preserved for us. As Baedeker repeats these imperial jests, however, I need not detail them.

Ghent Museum of Fine Arts

[Official webpage: http://www.mskgent.be/en/

Closed on Mondays, open between 10am and 6pm Tuesday to Sundays. Enquiries are taken via email: museum.msk@gent.be

This museum is located on the eastern side of the Citadelpark, a short 15 minute walk from Saint Peter's station.]

Given that its library of works dates from the 15th century onward, there is comparatively little by way of interest in the Ghent Museum of Fine Arts in the context of this handbook which is primarily occupied with Flemish Renaissance era works. There are however a few works displayed which are of interest, which I note herein. Should you be enthused about art of later periods, this gallery (formed to follow the unifying pattern of the Groeningemuseum in Bruges) has plenty to behold.

Ghent Museum of Fine Art - Image: Paul Hermans

The structure of the museum itself is in the main neoclassical in design, following the trends of the 19th century period to which it dates. It was designed by Charles van Rysselberghe, with construction finished shortly after 1900. Successive renovations, the latest of which concluded in 2007, have rendered the gallery's interior modern and quite bare aside from the portraiture within each room.

The works of Hieronymus Bosch receive a limited representation, with his Christ Carrying the Cross by far the most significant work on permanent display. Painted around 1510, the painting is a great jumble of faces wearing different expressions. Aside from these and the cross, there is no background as such – a conspicuous black envelops the scene in the painting's upper portions.

Some of the figures present are paying attention to the spectacle of Christ, others are seemingly distracted or engaged in their own business. Christ together with Veronica on the bottom left have closed their eyes, and wear plain and calm expressions in contrast to most of the faces around which are variously contorted. The image attempts and succeeds to contrast the serenity of faith with the chaos and hellishness of those without or apathetic toward belief.

In the Baroque sphere, a few notables likewise present themselves. Of good significance is Peter Paul Rubens *The Flagellation of Christ* – this is a sketch made in preparation for the full and complete work which today sits within St. Paul's Church in Antwerp. The later concluded work is part of the revered Antwerp canvas, in itself visual panoply of artistic achievement.

Additionally we have Anthony Van Dyck's Jupiter and Antiope. An early work by the artist, completed when he was merely twenty, the depiction is of the supreme God Jupiter making his intention of impregnating Antiope clear. The usual eagle watches intently, craning its neck if itself observing art, placing the viewer in the discomforting position of voyeur. For admirers of Anthony Van Dyck, this work has something of a milestone significance – betraying the young painter's evident imitation of his master Rubens, yet evidencing the wonderful talent yet to emerge in true splendour.

There are several less significant works of the Baroque era from lesser artists which can be readily beheld and interpreted. There is however one work of local significance to Ghent, being as it was commissioned by the Bishop Triest.

Theodore Rombouts *The Allegory of the Five Senses* is representative of the 17th century enthrallment with the allegorical. An era which advanced and chronicled so many of the folk tales we today enjoy, this fascination with the symbolic persists in our popular consciousness to this day.

The casual observer would see a group of friends, convivially enjoying a leisurely day of merriment. However, closer inspection reveals each gentleman to correspond to the five human senses of Sight, Sound, Taste, Touch and Smell. Thus the deceptively relaxed serenity actually carries greater meaning.

Historical Notes on Belgium

Within this series of guidebooks, separate Introductions to the various towns deal rather with their origins than offer a blow by blow historical account. I have laid stress chiefly on the industrial and municipal facts, which in Belgium are all-important. I add here, however, a few general notes on the political history of the country as a whole, with a chiefly dynastic bent. These may serve for reference, or at least as reminders; and in particular they should be useful as giving some information about the originals of portraits in the various galleries.

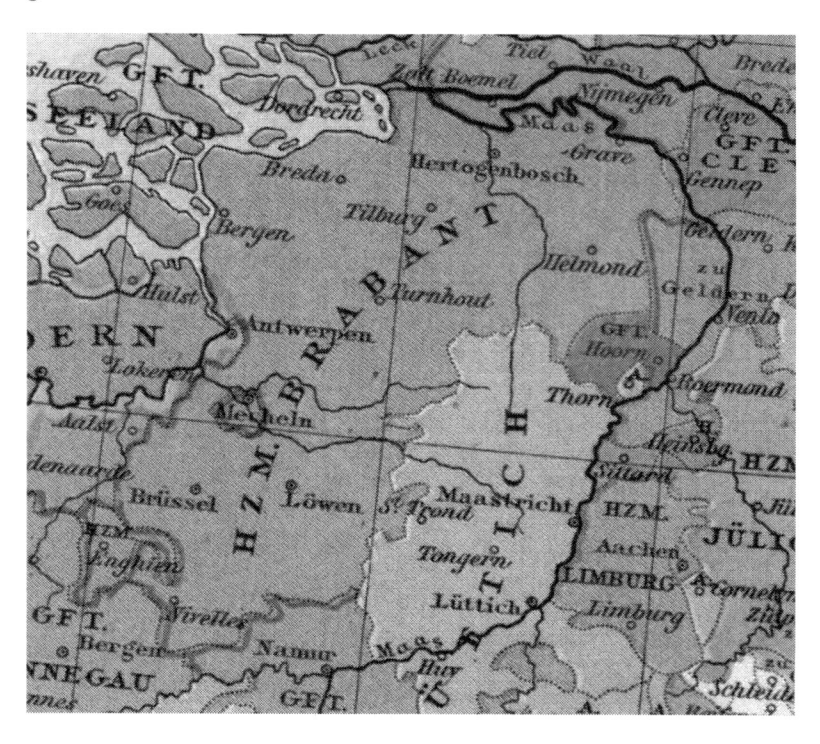

The two portions of the modern kingdom of Belgium with which we are most concerned in this Guide are the County of Flanders and the Duchy of Brabant. The first was originally a fief of France; the second, a component member of the Empire. They were commercially wealthier than the other portions of the Gallo-German borderland which is now Belgium; they were also the parts most affected by the Burgundian princes; on both which accounts, they are still by far the richest in works of art, alike in architecture, in painting, and in sculpture.

The vast Frankish dominions of the Merovingians and of the descendants of Charlemagne—of the Merwings and Karlings, to be more strictly Teutonic—showed at all times a tendency to break up into two distinct realms, known as the Eastern and Western Kingdoms (Austria—not, of course, in the modern sense—and Neustria). These kingdoms were not artificial, but based on a real difference of race and speech. The Eastern Kingdom (Franken or Franconia) where the Frankish and Teutonic blood was purest, became first the Empire, in the restricted sense, and later Germany and Austria (in part). The Western Kingdom (Neustria) where Celtic or Gallic blood predominated, and where the speech was Latin, or (later) French, became in time the Kingdom of France. But between these two Francias, and especially during the period of unrest, there existed a certain number of middle provinces, sometimes even a middle kingdom, known from its first possessor, Lothar, son of Charlemagne, as Lotharingia or Lorraine. Of these middle provinces, the chief northern members were Flanders, Brabant, Hainault, and Liège.

Flanders in the early Middle Ages was a fief of France; it included not only the modern Belgian provinces of East and West Flanders, but also French Flanders, that is to say the

Department of the Nord and part of the Pas de Calais. As early as the Treaty of Verdun (843), the land of Flanders was assigned to Neustria. But the county, as we know it, really grew up from the possessions of a noble family at Bruges and Sluys, the head of which was originally known as Forester or Ranger. In 862, the King of France, as suzerain, changed this title to that of Count, in the person of Baldwin Bras-de-Fer (Baldwin I.). Baldwin was also invested with the charge of the neighbouring coast of France proper, on tenure of defending it against the Norman pirates.

In 1006, his descendant, Baldwin IV., seized the Emperor's town of Valenciennes; and having shown his ability to keep his booty, he was invested by the Franconian Henry II. with this district as a fief, so that he thus became a feudatory both of France and of the Empire. He was also presented with Ghent and the Isles of Zealand. Baldwin V. (1036) added to the growing principality the districts of Alost, Tournai, and Hainault. The petty dynastic quarrels of the 11th century are far too intricate for record here; in the end, the domains of the Counts were approximately restricted to what we now know as Flanders proper. A bare list of names and dates must suffice for this epoch:—Baldwin V. (1036-1067); Baldwin VI. (1067-1070); Robert II. (1093-1111); and Baldwin VII. (1111-1119).

After this date, the native line having become extinct, the county was held by foreign elective princes, under whom the power of the towns increased greatly. Among these alien Counts, the most distinguished was Theodoric (in French, Thierry; in German, Dietrich; or in Dutch, Dierick) of Alsace, who was a distinguished Crusader, and the founder of the Chapel of the Holy Blood at Bruges (which see).

Under Baldwin of Hainault (1191-1194) Artois was ceded to France, together with St. Omer and Hesdin. Henceforth, Ghent superseded Arras as the capital. Baldwin IX. (1194-1206) became a mighty Crusader, and founded the Latin Empire of Constantinople. Indeed, the Crusades were largely manned and managed by Flemings. He was followed in Flanders by his two daughters, Johanna and Margaret, under whose rule the cities gained still greater privileges. Margaret's son, Guy de Dampierre, was the creature of Philippe IV. of France, who endeavoured to rule Flanders through his minister, Châtillon. The Flemings answered by just revolt, and fought the famous Battle of the Spurs near Courtrai, already described, against the French interlopers (see Bruges). In 1322, Louis de Nevers (Louis I.) became Count, and provoked by his Gallicising and despotic tendencies the formidable rebellion under Van Artevelde (see Ghent). The quarrel between the league of burghers and their lord continued more or less during the reigns of Count Louis II. (1346) and Louis III., who died in 1385, leaving one daughter, Margaret, married to Philip the Bold (Philippe-le-Hardi) of Burgundy.

The political revolution caused in Flanders and Brabant by the accession of the Burgundian dynasty was so deep-reaching that a few words must be devoted to the origin and rise of this powerful family, a branch of the royal Valois of France. The old Kingdom of Burgundy had of course been long extinct; but its name was inherited by two distinct principalities, the Duchy of Burgundy, which formed part of France, and the County of Burgundy (Franche Comté), which was a fief of the Empire. In the 14th century, a new middle kingdom, like the earlier Lotharingia, seemed likely to arise by the sudden growth of a practically independent power in this debatable land between France and Germany.

Anonymous portrait of John le Bon

In 1361, the Duchy of Burgundy fell in to the crown of France; and in order, as he thought, to secure its union with the central authority, John the Good of France (Jean-le-Bon), during the troublous times after the Treaty of Bretigny, conferred it as a fief upon his son, Philippe de Valois (Philip the Bold, or Philippe-le-Hardi) who married Margaret of Flanders, thus uniting two of the greatest vassal principalities of the French crown. In 1385, on the death of Louis III., Philip succeeded to the County of Flanders, now practically almost an independent state. After him reigned three other princes of his family.

John the Fearless (Jean-sans-Peur, 1404-1419) will be remembered by visitors to Paris as the builder of the Porte Rouge at Notre-Dame de Paris. Philip the Good (Philippe-le-Bon, 1419-1467) was the patron of Van Eyck and Memling. (His portrait by Roger van der Weyden is in the Antwerp Gallery.) Charles the Bold (Charles-le-Téméraire, 1467-1477) raised the power of the house to its utmost pitch, and then destroyed it. (His portrait by Memling is in the Brussels Gallery.) Contrary, however, to the belief of John the Good, the princes of the Valois dynasty in Burgundy, instead of remaining loyal to the crown of France, became some of its most dangerous and dreaded rivals.

All these Dukes, as French princes, played at the same time an important part in the affairs of France. They also won, by marriage, by purchase, by treaty, or by conquest, large territories within the Empire, including most of modern Belgium and Holland, together with much that is now part of France. They were thus, like their Flemish predecessors, vassals at once of the Emperor and the French king; but they were really more powerful than either of their nominal over-lords; for their central position between the two jealous neighbours gave them great advantages, while their possession of the wealthy cities of the Low Countries made them into the richest princes in mediæval Europe. It was at their opulent and ostentatious court that Van Eyck and Memling painted the gorgeous pictures which still preserve for us some vague memory of this old-world splendour. At the same time, the increased power of the princes, who could draw upon their other dominions to suppress risings in Flanders, told unfavourably upon the liberties of the cities. The Burgundian dominion thus sowed the seeds of the Spanish despotism.

Jean-sans-Peur was murdered by the Dauphin, afterwards Charles VII.; and this cousinly crime threw his son, Philippe-le-Bon, into the arms of the English. It was the policy of Burgundy and Flanders, indeed, to weaken the royal power by all possible means. Philip supported the English cause in France for many years; and it was his defection, after the Treaty of Arras in 1435, that destroyed the chances of Henry VI. on the Continent. The reign of Philippe-le-Bon, we saw, was the Augustan age of the Burgundian dynasty. (Fully to understand Burgundian art, however, you must visit Dijon as well as Brabant and Flanders.) Under Charles the Bold, the most ambitious prince of the Burgundian house, the power of the Dukes was raised for a time to its highest pitch, and then began to collapse suddenly. A constant rivalry existed between Charles and his nominal suzerain, Louis XI. It was Charles's dream to restore or re-create the old Burgundian kingdom by annexing Lorraine, with its capital, Nancy, and conquering the rising Swiss Confederacy.

He would thus have consolidated his dominions in the Netherlands with his discontinuous Duchy and County of Burgundy. He had even designs upon Provence, then as yet an independent county. Louis XI. met these attempts to create a rival state by a policy of stirring up enemies against his too powerful feudatory. In his war with the Swiss, Charles was signally defeated in the decisive battles at Granson and Morat, in 1476. In the succeeding year, he was routed and killed at Nancy, whither the Swiss had gone to help René, Duke of Lorraine, in his effort to win back his Duchy from Charles. The conquered Duke was buried at Nancy, but his body was afterwards brought to Bruges by his descendant, the Emperor Charles V., and now reposes in the splendid tomb which we have seen at Notre-Dame in that city.

This war had important results. It largely broke down the power of Burgundy. Charles's daughter, Mary, kept the Low Countries and the County of Burgundy (Imperial); but the Duchy (French) reverted to the crown of France, with which it was ever after associated. The scheme of a great Middle Kingdom thus came to an end; and the destinies of the Low Countries were entirely altered.

We have next to consider the dynastic events by which the Low Countries passed under the rule of the House of Hapsburg. In 1477, Mary of Burgundy succeeded her father Charles as Countess of Flanders, Duchess of Brabant, etc. In the same year she was married to Maximilian of Austria, King of the Romans, son of the Emperor Frederic III. (or IV.). Maximilian was afterwards elected Emperor on his father's death. The children of this marriage were Philip the Handsome (Philippe-le-Beau, or le-Bel; Philippus Stok), who died in 1506, and Margaret of Austria. Philip, again, married Johanna (Juana) the Mad, of Castile, and thus became King of Castile, in right of his wife. The various steps by which these different sovereignties were cumulated in the person of Philip's son, Charles V., are so important to a proper comprehension of the subject that I advise you seek out a family tree illustration in other to fully comprehend their significance and centrality.

During the lifetime of Maximilian, who was afterwards Emperor, Mary, and her son Philippe-le-Beau, ruled at first in the Low Countries (for the quarrel between Maximilian and Bruges over the tutorship of Philippe, see p. 27). After the death of Isabella of Castile, Ferdinand retired to Aragon, and Philippe ruled Castile on behalf of his insane wife, Juana. Philippe died in 1506, and his sister, Margaret of Austria, then ruled as Regent in the Netherlands (for Charles) till her death in 1530. Charles V., born at Ghent in 1500, was elected to the Empire after his grandfather, Maximilian I., and thus became at once Emperor, King of Spain, Duke of Austria, and ruler of the Low Countries.

(In 1516 he succeeded Ferdinand in the Kingdom of Spain, and in 1519 was elected Emperor.)

The same series of events carried the Netherlands, quite accidentally, under Spanish rule. For Charles was an absolutist, who governed on essentially despotic principles. His conduct towards Ghent in 1539 brought affairs to a crisis. The Emperor, in pursuance of his plans against France, had demanded an enormous subsidy from the city, which the burgesses constitutionally refused to grant, meeting the unjust extortion by open rebellion. They even entered into negotiations with François Ier; who, however, with the base instinct of a brother absolutist, betrayed their secret to his enemy the Emperor. Charles actually obtained leave from François to march a Spanish army through France to punish the Flemings, and arrived with a powerful force before the rebellious city. The Ghenters demanded pardon; but Charles, deeply incensed, entered the town under arms, and took up his abode there in triumph.

Alva, his ruthless Spanish commander (portrait in the Brussels Gallery), suggested that the town should be utterly destroyed; but the Emperor could not afford to part with his richest and most populous city, nor could even he endure to destroy his birth-place. He contented himself with a terrible vengeance, beheading the ringleaders, banishing the minor patriots, and forfeiting the goods of all suspected persons. The city was declared guilty of lèse-majesté, and the town magistrates, with the chiefs of the Guilds, were compelled to appear before Charles with halters round their necks, and to beg for pardon. The Emperor also ordered that no magistrate of Ghent should ever thenceforth appear in public without a halter, a badge which became with time a mere silken decoration. The privileges of the city were at the same time abolished, and the famous old bell, Roland, was removed from the Belfry.

Thenceforth Charles treated the Netherlands as a conquered Spanish territory. He dissolved the monastery of St. Bavon, and erected on its site the great Citadel, which he garrisoned with Spaniards, to repress the native love of liberty of the Flemings (see Ghent). In subsequent risings of the Low Countries, the Spaniards' Castle, the stronghold of the alien force, was the first point to be attacked; and on it depended the issue of freedom or slavery in the Netherlands. Charles also established the Inquisition, which is said to have put to death no fewer than 100,000 persons.

In 1555, the Emperor abdicated in favour of his son Philip, known as Philip II. of Spain. But his brother Ferdinand, to whom he had resigned his Austrian dominions, was elected Emperor (having been already King of the Romans) as Ferdinand I. From his time forth, the Empire became more exclusively German, so that its connexion with Rome was almost forgotten save as a historic myth, degenerating into the mere legal fiction of a Holy Roman Empire, with nothing Roman in it. Thus, the Netherlands alone of the earlier Burgundian heritage remained in the holding of the Austrian kings of Spain, who ruled them nominally as native sovereigns, but practically as Spaniards and aliens by means of imported military garrisons.

Philip II.—austere, narrow, domineering, fanatical—remained only four years in the Netherlands, and then retired to Spain, appointing his half-sister, Margaret of Parma (illegitimate daughter of Charles V.), regent of the Low Countries (1559-1567). She resided in the Ancienne Cour at Brussels. Her minister, Granvella, Bishop of Arras, made himself so unpopular, and the measures taken against the Protestants were so severe, that the cities, ever the strongholds of liberty, showed signs of revolution. They objected to the illegal maintenance of a Spanish standing army, and also to the Inquisition. In April, 1567, as a consequence of the discontents, the Duke of Alva was sent with 10,000 men as lieutenant-general to the Netherlands, to suppress what was known as the Beggars' League (Les Gueux), now practically headed by the Prince of Orange (William the Silent). Alva entered Brussels with his Spanish and Italian mercenaries and treacherously seized his two suspected antagonists, Count Egmont and Count Hoorn.

The patriotic noblemen were imprisoned at Ghent, in the Spaniards' Castle, were condemned to death, and finally beheaded in the Grand' Place at Brussels. (For fuller details of the great revolutionary movement thus inaugurated, see Motley's Rise of the Dutch Republic, and Juste's Le Comté d'Egmont et le Comté de Hornes.) Alva also established in Brussels his infamous "Council of Troubles," which put to death in cold blood no less than 20,000 inoffensive burghers. His cold and impassive cruelty led to the Revolt of the United Provinces in 1568—a general movement of all the Spanish Netherlands (as they now began to be called) to throw off the hateful yoke of Spain. Under the able leadership of William of Orange, the Flemings besieged and reduced the Spaniards' Castle at Ghent. In the deadly struggle for freedom which ensued, the Northern Provinces (Holland), aided by their great natural advantages for defence among the flooded marshes of the Rhine delta, succeeded in casting off their allegiance to Philip. They were then known as the United Netherlands. The long and heroic contest of the Southern Provinces (Belgium) against the Spanish oppressor was not equally successful.

A desperate struggle for liberty met with little result, and the Spanish sovereigns continued to govern their Belgian dominions like a conquered country. In 1578, Alessandro Farnese, Duke of Parma (son of Margaret), was sent as Governor to the Netherlands, where he remained in power till 1596. In the prosecution of the war against the Northern Provinces (Holland) he besieged Antwerp, and took it after fourteen months in 1585. In the "Spanish Fury" which followed, Antwerp was almost destroyed, and all its noblest buildings ruined. Nevertheless, under Parma's rule, the other cities recovered to a certain extent their municipal freedom; though the country as a whole was still treated as a vanquished province.

The next great landmark of Belgian history is the passage of the Spanish Netherlands under Austrian rule. The first indefinite steps towards this revolution were taken in 1598, when Philip II. ceded the country as a fief to his daughter the Infanta Isabella

(Clara Isabella Eugenia) on her marriage with Albert, Archduke of Austria, who held the provinces as the Spanish Governor. (Portraits of Albert and Isabella by Rubens in the Brussels Gallery.) The new rulers made the country feel to a certain extent that it was no longer treated as a mere disobedient Spanish appanage. After the troubles of the Revolt, and the cruel destruction of Antwerp by Parma, trade and manufactures began to revive.

Albert and Isabella were strongly Catholic in sentiment; and it was under their régime that the greater part of the rococo churches of Antwerp and other cities were built, in the showy but debased taste of the period, and decorated with large and brilliantly-coloured altar-pieces. They also induced Rubens to settle in the Netherlands, appointed him Court painter, and allowed him to live at Antwerp, where the trade of the Low Countries was still largely concentrated. During their vice-royalty, however, Brussels became more than ever the recognised capital of the country, and the seat of the aristocracy.

After Albert's death in 1621, the Netherlands reverted to Spain, and a dull period, without either art or real local history, supervened, though the wars of the 17th and 18th centuries were in great part fought out over these unfortunate provinces, "the cockpit of Europe."

The campaigns of Marlborough and Prince Eugene are too well-known as part of English and European history to need recapitulation here. At the end of the War of the Spanish Succession, the Peace of Rastadt, in 1714, assigned the Spanish Netherlands to Austria, thus entailing upon the unhappy country another hundred years of foreign domination.

Nevertheless, the Austrian Netherlands, as they were thenceforth called (in contradistinction to the "United Netherlands" or Holland), were on the whole tolerably well governed by the Austrian Stadtholders, who held their court at Brussels, and who were usually relations of the Imperial family. Few memorials, however, of Maria Theresa, of Joseph II., or of Léopold II. now exist in Belgium, and those few are not remarkable for beauty. It was during this relatively peaceful and law-abiding time, on the other hand, that the Upper Town of Brussels was laid out in its existing form by Guimard. As a whole, the Belgian provinces were probably better governed under Austrian rule than under any other régime up to the period of the existing independent and national monarchy.

The French Revolutionists invaded Belgium in 1794, and committed great havoc among historical buildings at Bruges and elsewhere. Indeed, they did more harm to the arts of the Netherlands than anybody else, except the Spaniards and the modern "restorers." They also divided Belgium into nine departments; and Napoleon half sneeringly, half cynically, justified the annexation on the ground that the Low Countries were the alluvial deposit of French rivers. The Belgian States formed part of Napoleon's composite empire till 1814, when these Southern Provinces were assigned by the Treaty of London to Holland. In 1815, during the Hundred Days, the Allied Armies had their headquarters at Brussels, and the decisive battle against Napoleon was fought at Waterloo. The Congress of Vienna once more affirmed the union of Belgium with Holland; they remained as one kingdom till the first revolutionary period in 1830.

The Southern Provinces then successfully seceded from the Dutch monarchy: indeed, the attempted fusion of semi-French and Catholic Belgium with purely Teutonic and Protestant Holland was one of those foredoomed failures so dear to diplomacy. A National Congress elected Léopold of Saxe-Coburg as King of the Belgians (Roi des Belges), and the crown is now held by his son, Léopold II. For nearly seventy years Belgium has thus enjoyed, for the first time in its history, an independent and relatively popular government of its own choosing. The development of its iron and coal industries during this epoch has vastly increased its wealth and importance; while the rise of Antwerp as a great European port has also done much to develop its resources. At the present day Belgium ranks as one of the most thickly populated, richest, and on the whole most liberal-minded countries of Europe. Its neutrality is assured by the Treaty of London, and its army exists only to repel invasion in case that neutrality should ever be violated.

Much of the country suffered greatly during the two World Wars of the 20th century. The First World War, which saw Belgium as a bulwark against the military offenses of the German Empire, saw great damage and bombardment upon the civic centres, with Antwerp particularly badly damaged in the conflict. Many towns, such as Ypres, would become inextricably associated with the carnage and conflict.

The famed retrieval of the Ghent altarpiece and its panels

The Second World War was, fortuitously, less damaging upon the many artistic and architectural attainments around the country. The occupied cities avoided catastrophic damage, the hardship mainly wrought by the citizenry rather than the established, physically manifest culture. Matters were both helped and hindered by the attention to art by the fascist invaders: while more fastidious with art than a typical aggressor, the Nazis would also set about hiding them. Over the course of years after the war, a large proportion of artworks were successfully restored or retrieved. Most notably of all was the retrieval of the Ghent Alterpiece from a salt mine in Altausee after the hostilities ended. Having been placed there by Axis forces under orders from Hitler, the recovered panels were displayed to great media attention at the time. The entire escapade was given a recent treatment in Hollywood, in the motion picture *The Monuments Men*.

Given the immensity and scale of the death, many soldiers and war dead were buried in Flanders. The area of Flanders Fields were particularly associated with the First World War, with the poppies growing there becoming synonymous with the bloodshed. An American cemetery bearing the name Flanders Field is where a total of 368 soldiers were buried, and has become a noted visitor destination for those interested in modern wartime history.

Across Belgian cities, comparatively faithful renovation projects ensued after the conclusion of World War 2. Accessibility to the major civic and cultural centres of Belgium became easier with the aid of modern advances in transportation, while dedicated art historians within and outside the city universities successfully brought the myriad artworks to justifiably good housing. Successive renovations, improved means of storage, and better education on the fragility of the works described – together with a general absence of conflict – mean the past seventy and more years have seen the twin Flemish treasures of art and architecture treated with relative fastidiousness. It is hoped that this happy state of affairs persists well into the 21st century and beyond, to the benefit and promulgation of fine art and culture.

Printed in Great Britain
by Amazon